| DATE DUE | | | |
|---|---|---|---|
| OCT 22 | | | |
| MAY 14 | | | |
| Mar. 4 | | | |
| Jan. 17 | | | |
| Jan. 31 | | | |
| | | | |
| | | | |
| | | | |
| | | | |
| | | | |
| | | | |
| | | | |
| | | | |
| | | | |
| | | | |
| | | | |

No. 370  Waverly Publishing Co.

# THE SUN

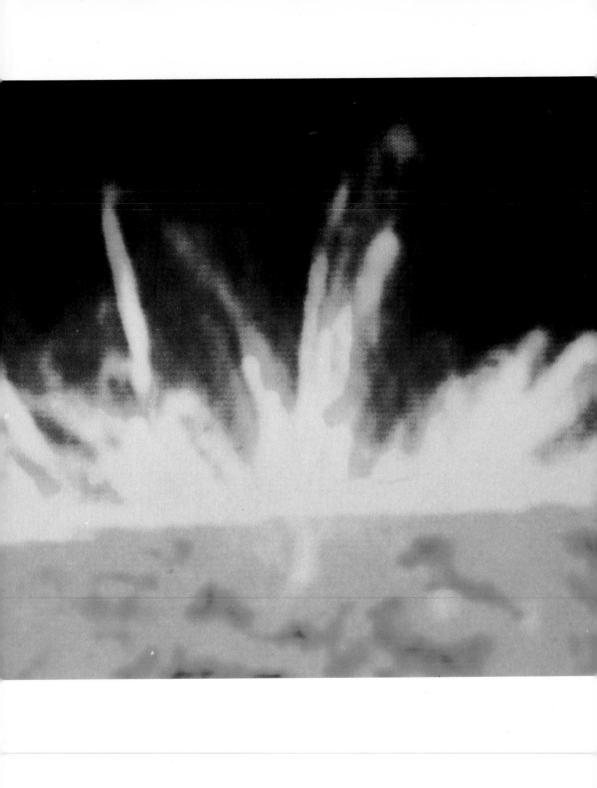

# THE SUN

## CHRISTOPHER LAMPTON

**FRANKLIN WATTS**
NEW YORK/LONDON/TORONTO/SYDNEY/1982
A FIRST BOOK

*FRONTIS: PHOTOGRAPH OF A CORONAL LOOP,
TAKEN BY A SPECIAL CAMERA.*

Cover photograph courtesy of NASA

Diagrams by Vantage Art, Inc.

Interior photographs courtesy of the Harvard
College Observatory: p. ii; The Bettmann Archive,
Inc.: pp. 13, 14, 17, 20; the New York Public
Library Picture Collection: p. 23; NASA: pp. 29,
37, 39, 42, 45, 52, 63; Hansen Planetarium/
© 1979 Richard A. Keen: p. 35; and the Amer-
ican Museum of Natural History: p. 55.

Library of Congress Cataloging in Publication Data

Lampton, Christopher.
The sun.

(A First book)
Bibliography: p.
Includes index.
Summary: Discusses the formation, composition,
and movement of the sun and explains the importance
of this star to life on Earth.
1. Sun—Juvenile literature. [1. Sun] I. Title.
QB521.5.L35      523.7      81-21991
ISBN 0-531-04390-8                AACR2

# CONTENTS

# THE SUN

# *PREFACE*

Our sun has been shining for 5 billion years.

The sun is older than history, older than the human race, older than life itself. The same sun that shone on the dinosaurs and on the ancient Egyptians shines on us today.

Without the sun there would *be* no history, no human race, no life. The sun gives us food and fuel, wind and rain. Without the sun the earth would be a lifeless rock wandering through space.

Thousands of years ago, the sun was worshiped as a god. Today we know that the sun is a natural phenomenon, no different in kind from the burning of a match or the explosion of a hydrogen bomb.

This is a book about the sun and what it means in the lives of human beings. We may no longer worship the sun as a god. But the role that it plays in our lives is no less great.

# CHAPTER ONE
# THE
# PERFECT LIGHT

Imagine that you lived in a world where once a year the sun threatened to disappear forever.

Suppose that in this imaginary world the sun drifted southward for months at a time, moving closer and closer to the horizon. As the sun wandered away, it would take its light and warmth with it. The world would grow dark and cold.

The inhabitants of such a world would live in fear of losing the sun forever. What if it never came back? What if the sun drifted over the horizon and vanished from sight, never to return? A long winter's night would settle over the world. Crops would die. Rivers would freeze. Eventually, all life would cease to exist.

Now, imagine that once a year the sun of our imaginary world returns. Its southward movement gradually comes to a halt. Slowly it reverses its course, bringing light and warmth back with it.

What would the inhabitants of such a world do? What would *you* do on the day the sun began to return?

Most likely, you would throw a party.

In fact, you probably do just this, though you may not realize that you're celebrating the return of the sun.

The world we've just described is our own. Throughout the summer and fall, our sun wanders farther and farther southward. (Actually, it just *seems* to do this. It is really the earth that changes its position relative to the sun, not vice versa.) In the northern hemisphere, the days grow shorter, the weather colder. Just when it looks as though the sun may drift horizon-ward forever, it stops and begins to return.

The day that the sun starts moving northward again is called the *winter solstice*. Today, we more commonly refer to this date as the "first day of winter." It falls on or about the twenty-first day of December (though the ancient Romans, among others, believed the solstice came on December 25).

Several holidays fall in the month of December—Christmas, Hanukkah, New Year's Eve. For most of us, this is a time of parties and celebration. This tradition of December festivities, however, goes back thousands of years. On December 25, the ancient Romans celebrated the Feast of *Sol Invictus* —"the Unconquerable Sun"—in honor of the winter solstice. It's no accident that this is also the date on which we celebrate Christmas. The early Christian Church was established most firmly among the Romans, many of whom had only lately been converted from the worship of pagan gods. These early converts frequently mixed their worship of Christ with pagan rituals, celebrating the Feast of *Sol Invictus* along with the Christian holidays. To remove the pagan significance from the solstice celebration, the officials of the Church adopted December 25 as the date of the Christmas celebration, though it does not say in the Bible that Christ was born on this date.

So, in a very real sense, the Christmas holiday is a celebration in honor of the returning sun.

Is it any wonder that ancient civilizations worshiped the sun as a god? Even primitive humans must have been aware of the sun's importance. Life could not exist without it.

In ancient Egypt, there were more than half a dozen different sun gods. There was the god of the setting sun and the god of the rising sun. There was the god of the sun's disk and the god of the sun's rays. There was even the god of the sun's heat

*Akhenaten and his wife showing their adoration of the sun.*

*The Incas worship the sun.*

and the god of the sun's light. The pharaoh (or king) of Egypt was believed to be a descendant of one of these gods. One pharaoh, Amenhotep IV, put an end to the worship of multiple gods in Egypt and declared that henceforth there would be only one true god—Aten, god of the sun's disk. Amenhotep even changed his name to Akhenaten—"pleasing to Aten." Akhenaten died young, though, and after his death the Egyptians returned to worshiping the old gods.

The Inca Indians of South America believed that their king was descended from the sun. The entire life-style of the Incas revolved around sun worship. Many Incan buildings were carefully positioned on the eastern slopes of mountains so that the first rays of the rising sun could be seen from every house at dawn. The Inca citizens would rise early to offer prayers to their god as he appeared above the horizon.

Yet even as some people worshiped the sun as a god, others studied it using the methods of science, just as they would any other natural phenomenon. The ancient Babylonians, for instance, carefully recorded the movements of the sun in relation to other heavenly bodies—the stars, the moon, and the planets. However, the Babylonians believed that the sun and planets had a profound influence on earthly events. For instance, it was thought that the position of the sun in relation to the stars at a child's birth would shape the child's life and character. This belief is called *astrology* and still persists to this day. Horoscope columns in the daily newspapers offer advice based on the position of the sun at the time of your birth. There is no scientific evidence, however, that astrology is anything more than superstition.

Though the Babylonians contributed much to our knowledge of the sun's movements, no attempt was made to study the true nature of the sun until the time of the ancient Greeks, about 2,400 years ago.

Around 434 B.C., the Greek astronomer Anaxagoras suggested that the sun was a mass of burning stone larger than the Peloponnesus, the peninsula of land on which much of Greece rested. In addition, Anaxagoras claimed that this mass of stone was about 4,000 miles (6,400 km) away.

Actually, the sun is about 93 million miles (148.8 million km) away, but Anaxagoras arrived at his conclusion through solid scientific reasoning. Unfortunately, this reasoning was based on incorrect data.

Another Greek astronomer, Aristarchus of Samos, made a somewhat better estimate of the distance to the sun. He based his estimate on the apparent relation of the sun and moon in the sky and the way the sun's light lit up the moon's surface. By mathematically computing the angles formed by the sun, moon, and earth when the moon was exactly half-full, it was possible for Aristarchus to work out the distance from the earth to both the moon and sun. His estimate of the moon's distance was surprisingly accurate. His estimate of the sun's distance, however, fell considerably short.

Most Greeks, even the Greek scientists, believed that the earth was the center of the universe and that the sun revolved around it. One can easily understand this belief. The sun *looks* as though it orbits the earth. Yet Aristarchus proposed a different theory, that the earth and all of the other planets orbit the sun. The sun, then, would be the center of the universe. This is sometimes called the *heliocentric* ("sun-centered") *model of the universe*. All of this went against certain religious beliefs of the time, however, and Aristarchus was accused of heresy. He was forced to leave his hometown in Greece and live elsewhere. His theories failed to catch on.

Science advanced little in the years after the Greeks. The idea that the sun went around the earth persisted for hundreds of years. It was not until the sixteenth century A.D. that anyone dared to revive the heliocentric model. The scientist who did so was Nicolaus Copernicus, born in Poland in 1473. Copernicus was a mathematician who was interested in the way the universe worked. After much study, he became convinced that Aristarchus had been right, that the earth and the other planets did revolve around the sun.

*Nicolaus Copernicus, 1473–1543*

Copernicus, however, hesitated to publish his theory. He was aware of what had happened to Aristarchus more than eighteen centuries earlier. He knew that the Church of the sixteenth century would no more welcome the idea of a heliocentric universe than did the religious authorities of Aristarchus's day. Nevertheless, he wrote a book entitled *De Revolutionibus Orbium Celestium* ("On the Revolutions of the Celestial Spheres"). In it, he described how the earth and the other planets that were known at the time (Mercury, Venus, Mars, Jupiter, and Saturn) revolved around the sun. Only the moon revolved around the earth. Taken together, all of these heavenly bodies came to be known as the *solar* ("sun") *system*.

Copernicus's book was published on the very day he died. According to legend, he saw a copy of it only once, while on his deathbed. Thus, Copernicus escaped the fate of Aristarchus.

Why did Copernicus fear the Church?

According to the religion of the sixteenth century, the universe was created directly by the hand of God, just as a watch is created by the hands of a watchmaker. Because God is perfect, reasoned the officials of the Church, the universe had to be perfect also.

Part of this perfection was that the earth must be at the center of the universe, or so the reasoning went. Copernicus's theories were in defiance of this idea. Eventually, the Church was to cause one man, Giordano Bruno, to be burned at the stake for preaching the theory of the heliocentric universe. Little wonder, then, in an atmosphere such as this, that Copernicus was frightened.

Another part of the perfect-universe doctrine was that every individual element of the universe had to be perfect, just as every element of a perfect watch would be perfect. And if every element of the universe was perfect, then the sun must be perfect, too.

There was only one problem.

It wasn't.

—18

# CHAPTER TWO
# THE
# IMPERFECT LIGHT

No one knows exactly when the telescope was invented, but it was probably sometime early in the seventeenth century. When word of its invention reached the Italian astronomer Galileo Galilei, he promptly built a telescope of his own—and so began a revolution in the science of astronomy.

This was in 1609. Galileo wasted no time in turning his small instrument skyward. Within a year he had published a book detailing many of his discoveries.

One of the things that Galileo saw through his telescope were spots on the surface of the sun. He was not the first to notice these *sunspots*. They had been reported by Chinese astronomers 2,000 years before.

Nonetheless, Galileo's announcement of sunspots caused a stir among those who believed that the sun was the flawless handiwork of God. The Church was infuriated. It also rankled under Galileo's insistence that the heliocentric model of the universe was the correct one. Eventually, Galileo was forced to deny his own discoveries and ideas about the "imperfection" of God's creations, particularly the idea that the earth revolved around the sun. The Roman Catholic Church of Galileo's time was very powerful.

But not so powerful that it could stifle truth forever. Galileo had been silenced, but the idea that the earth revolved around the sun lived on. In the years after Galileo's death, the

Galileo Galilei, 1564–1642

heliocentric model of the universe became accepted as essentially correct. (Actually, the sun is *not* at the center of the universe. It is one of many suns, or stars, that you can see in the sky on a clear night. Still, the sun is at the center of the solar system, and to that extent the heliocentric model was an accurate one.)

It was Sir Isaac Newton who, in 1687, finally showed why the solar system worked the way it did. All matter, said Newton, possessed a property called *gravitation* (or, more simply, *gravity*). Gravity is an *attractive* force. That is, any object that has gravitation (as all objects do) will attract other objects. The larger and more massive the object, the more of this attraction it will have.

The earth, for instance, is quite large and massive. It follows, then, that its gravitational attraction is very strong. This is why, if you jump up in the air, you always fall back to earth. The earth's gravity pulls you back. Smaller objects—books, houses, even people—have gravity, too. But compared to the earth, their gravity is very weak. In fact, it is detectable only by sensitive instruments.

Gravity is what holds the solar system together. It is the "glue" that keeps the planets from flying away into outer space, leaving the sun far behind. The sun, being extremely large and massive, has more gravitational attraction than all of the planets put together.

Why don't the planets simply fall into the sun since they are attracted by its gravity? Because the sun's gravitational attraction is balanced out by something called *centrifugal force*. This is a force that tends to impel an object or body outward from a center of rotation. In this case, the centrifugal force is caused by the sideways motion of the planets in relation to the sun. There is no room here for a detailed explanation of centrifugal force, but you can demonstrate it for yourself by tying a small rock to the end of a string and whirling it around in circles. As it whirls around, the rock will be very much like a small planet, with you as the sun and the string playing the role of gravity. The sideways motion of the rock— the centrifugal force, in other words—will cause it to tug away from you. The string will keep it from escaping.

By showing that gravitation was a universal force—that is, a force that exists everywhere, between all objects—Newton proved once and for all that the theories of Aristarchus and Copernicus had a sound basis.

After the invention of the telescope, our knowledge of the sun expanded by leaps and bounds. For instance, by studying the light from the sun in a device called a *spectrograph*, it became possible to tell what the sun was made up of. We know now that it consists mostly of two gases, hydrogen and helium.

Nonetheless, the sun still kept its secrets. The main question that solar astronomers now asked was, why does the sun keep burning? What is its fuel? Until the end of the last century, no one really knew.

In the middle of the nineteenth century, a scientist named Hermann Ludwig Ferdinand von Helmholtz began looking for the source of the sun's heat. His reasoning probably went something like this:

The sun seemed to be burning. It produced light and heat, much like a burning log or burning coal. Therefore, the sun had to be some kind of fire.

But what was doing the burning? Logs? Coal?

If the sun were made of burning coal, it would have been nothing more than ashes after a few thousand years. History tells us that the sun had burned much longer than that. Therefore, it was not made of burning coal. There were kinds of fuel that might keep the sun burning for longer than this, but not as long as history required.

Helmholtz had another idea based on a theory first suggested by Julius Mayer in 1848. If the sun were a mass of burning material, perhaps it was receiving a constant supply of

*Hermann Ludwig Ferdinand von Helmholtz, 1821–1894*

"fuel." He knew that the earth's atmosphere was often struck by meteors, chunks of rock or metal from outer space that glow white-hot as they pass through the earth's atmosphere. (This heat is caused by friction with the air.) If enough meteors fell into the sun, this might keep the sun constantly resupplied with burnable material. Furthermore, these meteors would grow hot from frictional heat as they passed through the helium and hydrogen gases that make up the sun. This additional heat would greatly increase the heat of the sun.

But alas, Helmholtz had some idea of how many meteors were floating around in space, and it didn't seem to him like enough. On top of this, meteors falling into the sun would make the sun grow larger. As it grew larger, its gravity would increase. And as its gravity increased, the earth would be more strongly attracted to it. The earth's orbit would grow smaller. If the earth's orbit grew smaller, the year would become shorter. Each year, in fact, would be two seconds slower than the one before. There was no evidence at all that this was happening. Therefore, the sun's heat did not come from meteors.

Undaunted, Helmholtz developed yet another theory. Suppose that our sun had formed from a giant cloud of gas. (This makes sense, as the sun is mostly hydrogen and helium, which are gases.) This gas cloud would have been made up of extremely small particles called *atoms.* (Nearly everything in the universe is made up of atoms, including living creatures. Atoms are the basic building blocks from which everything is constructed.)

Just as the earth and the sun have gravitational attraction, so do atoms. (In fact, the gravitational attraction of a planet or star is nothing more than the sum total of the gravitational attraction of all the atoms that make it up.) Atoms, however, are very small, and the gravity of an individual atom is very weak. Still, in a large cloud of gas, every atom would have a small attraction over every other atom. In time, they would drift closer together, and the cloud would grow smaller.

—24

As the atoms came together, though, they would tend to bump into one another. Maybe you've seen what happens when you strike two rough stones together. Hot sparks fly. (As with the falling meteors, this heat is caused by friction.) In the same way, these atoms would heat up when they ran into one another.

This heat, Helmholtz thought, might be the source of the sun's energy. Perhaps the sun was a glowing cloud of hot gas, its heat created by collisions between atoms as the cloud contracted.

There was, however, a problem. This kind of contractional gravitational heat would be enough to keep the sun burning for about 18 million years. This sounds like a long time, but not all scientists believed it was long enough.

Geologists are scientists who study the earth. They had evidence, they said, that the earth had been around longer than 18 million years—much longer, in fact. How could the earth be older than the sun?

At the end of the nineteenth century, no one knew of an energy source stronger than gravitational heat. Yet there *was* one. And the key to the mystery lay at the heart of the atom itself.

# CHAPTER THREE
# THE SECRET
# OF THE SUN

What is the world made of?

This might seem like a simple question. Obviously, the world is made of rocks and water and air and dirt and all of the other things that we see around us every day. Yet there is another answer to this question.

Pick up a rock. It certainly seems like a solid object. If someone asked you what the rock was made of, you might reply that it was made of rock. What else would it be made of?

And yet, if you strike the rock against the hard pavement of the sidewalk, it might break down into smaller rocks. The answer to the question, then, might be that big rocks are made of smaller rocks. And if you crush these small rocks with a hammer, they will crumble until the fragments of rock look pretty much like dirt. (This is, in fact, one of the ways in which dirt is formed.) Another answer to the question, then, is that rocks are made up of dirt.

If you think about this, however, it might occur to you that the pieces of dirt can be broken up into still smaller pieces of dirt, and so on. Is there any limit as to how small a piece you can break the rock into?

Yes. Eventually, the pieces of dirt would fall apart into particles called atoms, the same particles that we looked at in chapter two. (Actually, it would take special instruments to break a rock apart into atoms. You probably couldn't do it on your sidewalk.) The atom, as we have seen, is the basic building block of the universe. Everything is made up of atoms, with a few *very* rare exceptions. The atom is extremely small, so small that it cannot be seen with the eye, even through a microscope. Special electronic instruments can take fuzzy pictures of very large atoms; otherwise, they are more or less invisible.

One of the first people to suggest that matter was made up of atoms was the Greek philosopher Democritus, who lived around 430 B.C. Like his countryman Aristarchus, Democritus was largely ignored, even laughed at, for his beliefs. It was only in the twentieth century that the philosophy of *atomism* really became acceptable.

Is the atom simply a hard chunk of matter, like an extremely small grain of sand? No. In fact, it is possible to break atoms into still smaller pieces, just as we can break a rock into smaller pieces. These pieces are called *subatomic particles.*

Every atom is made up of subatomic particles. However, not all atoms are alike. In fact, there are many different kinds of atoms. Each one has a name. The air that you breathe, for instance, is made up of atoms of oxygen, nitrogen, carbon, and others. These particular atoms are called *gases* because at room temperature they take the form of a gas. (This kind of gas is not the same as the gas, or gasoline, that goes into the tank of an automobile.) Other kinds of atoms are solid at room temperature—iron, for instance, or tin.

The difference between these atoms is in how many subatomic particles they contain. Some atoms contain more subatomic particles than others.

The simplest kind of atom is hydrogen. It is a gas, like the air we breathe. The hydrogen atom is made up of only two subatomic particles.

When hydrogen atoms get extremely hot, they become jumbled together. The subatomic particles in the atoms combine. When this happens, the hydrogen atoms become a *different* kind of atom. They become helium atoms, which are the second simplest kind of atom. Helium is also a gas.

This combining process is called *hydrogen fusion*. We say that the hydrogen atoms *fused* into helium atoms.

Something else happens when hydrogen atoms fuse together. Energy is released.

Energy is what makes things move. The food that you eat contains energy, which is why you are able to move. The gasoline that you put into a car contains energy. Energy takes many forms. One of these forms is heat. Another is light. (You might wonder what these have to do with making things move. Heat, however, is what drives a steam engine, such as the ones on old-fashioned locomotives—and a locomotive certainly moves. And light can produce heat, as anyone who has stood in the sun on a summer day can tell you. Properly focused, light can make water boil, and the energy from that boiling water can drive a steam engine!)

The energy that is released when hydrogen atoms fuse is in the form of gamma rays. Gamma rays are a kind of radiation invisible to the eye. They are extremely hot.

The hydrogen bomb is the most powerful weapon ever invented. In a hydrogen bomb explosion, hydrogen atoms fuse into helium atoms. Gamma rays are released. A powerful wave of energy shoots outward from the center of the explosion, destroying everything in its path. Light and heat are produced.

What does this have to do with the sun?

Well, we know that the sun is very hot, hot enough for hydrogen atoms to combine into helium atoms, releasing gamma rays. And we know that gamma rays are an excellent source of heat energy.

Is it possible then that the sun is simply a gigantic hydrogen bomb exploding in outer space? In a sense, that is exactly what it is. At the center of the sun, it is hot enough for hydrogen atoms to combine (fuse) into helium atoms. This produces

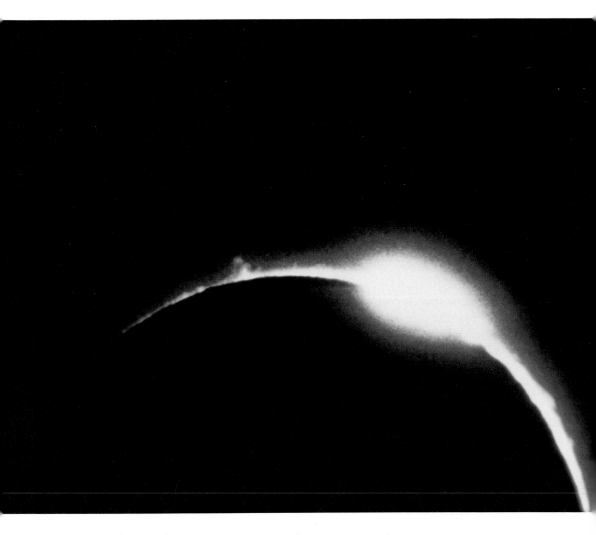

*The so-called Diamond Ring effect seen during an eclipse of the sun. The effect is caused by the last bright rays of sunlight shining through mountain peaks on the moon just before the moon moves in front of the sun and completely covers its disk.*

gamma rays, which in turn produce heat and light. (We'll see how this happens in the next chapter.)

But how did this explosion get started? Hydrogen fusion wouldn't have begun unless things were very hot in the first place. But where did this heat come from?

Helmholtz believed that the sun got its heat from contractional friction between atoms. He was half right. It was this that caused the sun to become hot in the first place. But then hydrogen fusion began—and kept the sun burning for billions of years! At last scientists had an explanation for the sun's heat that satisfied both astronomers and geologists.

With this in mind, let's take a look at how the sun was probably born.

About 5 billion years ago, where the sun is now, a cloud of gas floated in space. Such clouds were very common then—and still are. Even today, we can see many of them through our telescopes, floating between the stars.

The gas in the cloud was mostly hydrogen. Hydrogen is made up of atoms. Each atom has a small amount of gravitational attraction. The atoms attracted one another and therefore came closer together. The cloud shrunk. The atoms bumped into one another, and this created heat through friction. The cloud became hot and started to glow, just as the burner on an electric stove glows as it heats up.

When a certain temperature was reached, the hydrogen atoms began to fuse. The cloud began to expand, or explode, like a huge hydrogen bomb. Now there were two forces at work in the cloud—gravity, which pulled the atoms of gas closer together, and fusion, which blew them apart. These two forces balanced each other out, like two equal teams in a tug-of-war.

The cloud settled into the shape of a giant sphere, or globe. Energy shot away from the sphere in various forms of light and heat.

And a star—our sun—was born!

# CHAPTER FOUR
## THE
## PEACEFUL SUN

What is the sun like?

For starters, it is very *big*! It has a diameter of 865,000 miles (1,384,000 km), or 108 times the diameter of the earth. If the sun were a hollow ball, 1.3 million earths would fit inside it! The sun is that huge.

And yet, as stars go, the sun is only medium-sized. We would be safe in calling it an average star. There are other stars hundreds and thousands of times larger than our sun.

Such stars are fairly rare, however, because they use up their hydrogen "fuel" very quickly. Most stars are smaller than the sun. These stars burn for hundreds of billions of years. Large stars, on the other hand, may burn for only a few hundred thousand years. Our sun will probably burn for around 10 billion years in all.

Because of its relatively small size and yellowish color, astronomers classify the sun as a *yellow dwarf.* It is one of 100 billion stars that make up a vast cloud of stars called the *Milky Way.* And the Milky Way is only one of millions, perhaps billions, of *galaxies*, each containing billions of stars. Our galaxy is so large that light would take 100,000 years to cross it. Compared to the size of our galaxy, the sun is very small indeed.

Still, to human beings, the sun is large enough. It produces all the light and heat that we need. Its gravity keeps our planet from flying off into the emptiness of space.

# The Structure of the Sun

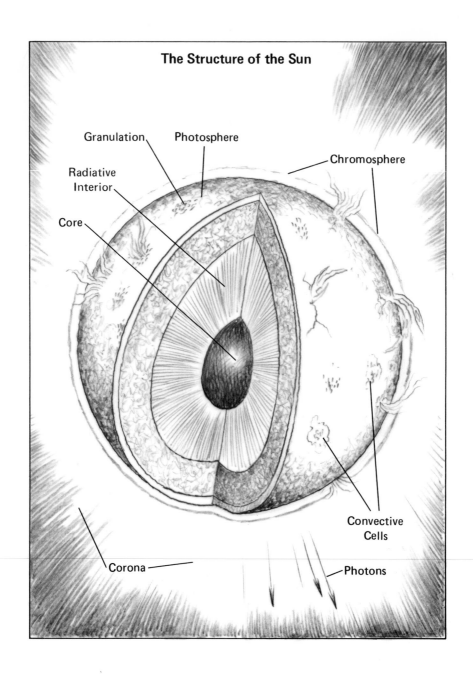

Granulation

Photosphere

Chromosphere

Radiative
Interior

Core

Convective
Cells

Corona

Photons

If we could take a trip to the sun, all the way to its center and back out again, what would we see?

Such a trip is impossible, of course, at least at the moment. Any material known would be destroyed instantly by the temperatures inside the sun. But we can imagine that we have a spaceship strong enough to withstand the heat and instruments that would let us "see" while we were inside the sun.

Let's start our journey at the center of the sun and work outward. At the very center is an area about as big as the planet Jupiter, called the sun's *core*. This is where hydrogen fuses into helium. The temperature at the core is 27,000,000° F (15,000,000°C). The hydrogen fusion that takes place here produces large amounts of gamma rays. These gamma rays *radiate* (move outward in all directions) from the core. Because they radiate, we can say that these gamma rays are a form of *radiation*.

Although gamma rays are a form of radiation, we saw earlier that they are invisible. Therefore, the sun's core is a very dark place, which is surprising. As we moved through the center of the sun in our imaginary spaceship, we would see only darkness through our windows. But if we had special instruments that would let us "see" the gamma rays, the sun's core would be dazzlingly bright.

Normally, gamma rays move very fast, at the speed of light in fact. (Light travels at 186,300 miles [239,280 km] per second, faster than anything else known.) But the gas at the center of the sun is very dense—that is, very tightly packed. It is about a hundred times denser than most metals. The gamma rays bounce back and forth between the tightly packed atoms, struggling to make their way to the sun's surface. They eventually succeed, but they are so slowed down by the dense gases that the journey takes *10 million years!*

The gamma rays move outward through the largest portion of the sun, the *radiative interior*. As they travel, they go through a slow change. Instead of invisible gamma rays, they become visible rays of light as well as other kinds of radiation, including ultraviolet, radio, infrared, and X rays.

The sun's light is extremely hot. It heats the outer layers of the sun until they begin to glow. Superheated sections form near the surface of the sun, just as bubbles form in boiling water and for pretty much the same reasons. These are called *convective cells.*

The outer layer of the sun is known as the *photosphere* ("sphere of light"). The photosphere is what we see when we look at the sun from the earth. The temperature of the photosphere is about 10,000°F (5,500°C).

Viewed through a powerful telescope, we can see the convective cells rising to the sun's surface. They look like speckles or grains of rice on the photosphere. We call these speckles *granulation.*

Light and heat from the photosphere escape into space in the form of waves. These waves are made up of actual particles of light called *photons.* Photons carry the sun's energy through space at 186,300 miles (298,080 km) per second. They cross the 93 million miles (148.8 million km) between the sun and the earth in about eight minutes.

Like the earth, the sun has an "atmosphere," a cloud of gases around its "surface." (Because the sun itself is made of gas, it's hard to say where the sun ends and the atmosphere begins. When we talk about the sun's surface, though, we usually mean the photosphere.) These gases are hot and shining, but they are usually invisible from earth, lost in the glare of the photosphere. They can, however, be viewed with special instruments. They can also be viewed during an *eclipse.* An eclipse takes place when the moon moves in front of the sun's

*The sun in total eclipse*

—34

disk, so that *only* the atmosphere is visible. (However, you should *never* stare directly at the sun, even during an eclipse. Doing so can cause blindness.)

The lowest level of the sun's atmosphere is called the *chromosphere* ("sphere of colors"), because it glows with a faint pinkish light. Its thickness varies, but on the average it is about 6,000 miles (9,600 km) in depth. The upper portion of the chromosphere is broken up into a series of sharp points called *spicules.* Through a telescope, these spicules have been described as looking like a "field of waving wheat." These fiery, gaseous fingers sometimes reach far into the outer layer of the sun's atmosphere.

This outer layer, which surrounds the chromosphere, is called the *corona.* During an eclipse, the corona is visible as a halo, or crown, of light. In fact, the word *corona* means "crown."

The corona extends great distances into space, stretching outward for millions of miles. The gases in the corona are much hotter than those in the chromosphere. Temperatures here rise into the millions of degrees. Of course, the gases in the corona are very thin (many times thinner than the air that we breathe on earth), and therefore little heat is needed to raise these gases to high temperatures. Still, the corona is very hot, and we are not yet sure why this is so.

The picture of the sun that we have just drawn might be called the "peaceful sun"—if anything this hot and dynamic can be called peaceful. There is, however, another face to the sun, one that is even more turbulent. We call that sun the "violent sun."

To understand how the sun can be violent, let's take a look at electricity and magnetism.

You probably know what electricity is. At least you know that it is what comes out of an electric socket. If you plug a lamp into the socket, the electricity flows into the lamp through the

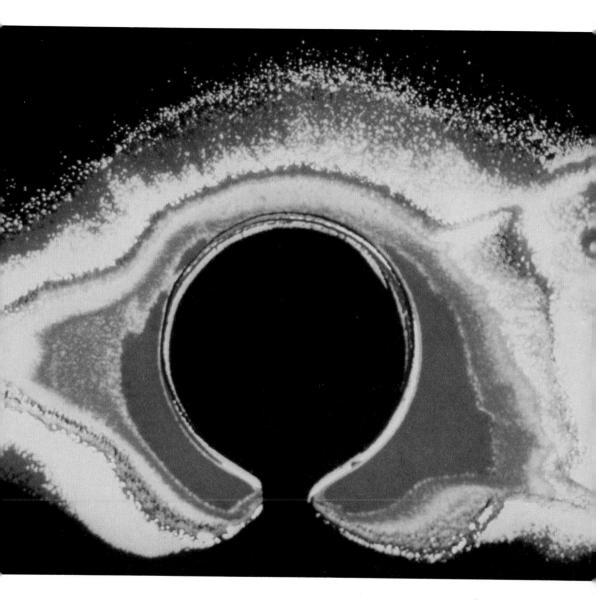

*A special solar telescope aboard Skylab 3 took
this picture of the sun's inner and outer coronas.*

cord and lights the bulb. Electricity, like light and heat, is a form of energy. It can be used to make things move—an electric motor, for instance.

You probably also know what magnetism is. Even a small magnet, such as the horseshoe magnets that you may have seen or played with, can pick up certain metal objects—nails and paper clips, for instance, or any small object consisting mainly of iron or steel. A large magnet can pick up refrigerators and cars. The *magnetic force* is very powerful.

Electricity and magnetism are very closely related. The reason for this has to do with the particles that make up the atom. We saw earlier that the atom is made up of subatomic particles. Some of these particles, especially the electrons, can be affected by magnetic force. That is, a magnet can reach out and grab these particles, causing them either to move toward the magnet or away from it.

Ordinarily, though, these particles are locked away safely inside the atom. They cannot be affected by magnets. Atoms are not affected by magnets either, at least not under normal conditions.

Sometimes, however, an atom can lose some of its electrons. Then the atom can be affected by magnets. The loose electrons can be affected by magnets, too. An atom that loses one or more of its electrons is called an *ion*. Ions are subject to magnetic force.

What does this have to do with electricity?

*The bright points of light appearing on this solar telescope photograph of the sun overlie regions of strong solar magnetism.*

—38

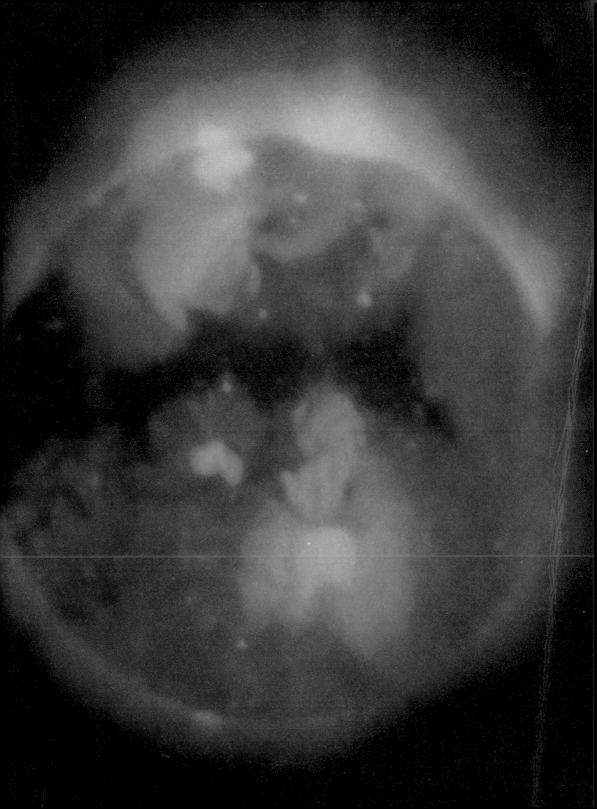

Well, you'll notice that the name *electron* sounds a lot like the word *electricity*. In fact, electricity is nothing more than the flow of electrons, just as a river is nothing more than the flow of water. When you plug a lamp into a socket, those incredibly tiny particles race through the cord and into the bulb.

Under the right conditions, this flow of electrons can create a magnet. For example, have you ever heard of a device called an electromagnet? An electromagnet is a magnet created by running electrons through a special coil of wire. This sets up a flow of electricity, which in turn creates a magnetic force. (Actually, scientists like to refer to magnetism as the *electro*magnetic force, because of its relationship to electricity.) The area around the electromagnet becomes what is called a *magnetic field.* A magnetic field is an area in space filled with electromagnetic force. An iron or steel object in this field will be instantly gripped by the magnet. A large electromagnet can lift objects weighing many tons.

When an atom loses an electron and becomes an ion, it can be affected by these magnetic fields.

Under certain conditions, magnetic fields occur on the surface of the sun. These fields are often more powerful than any ever produced on earth. In fact, they are more powerful than all of the magnetic fields on earth put together—*much* more powerful.

There are also ions on the sun. When these ions get together with these powerful magnetic fields, the result is . . . explosive.

# CHAPTER FIVE
# THE
# VIOLENT SUN

Galileo announced his sighting of sunspots in the seventeenth century, yet they still puzzle scientists today. What are these strange dark patches on the sun?

As seen through a telescope, sunspots are just that—dark patches on the sun, almost always found in pairs. Actually, they aren't even dark, just darker—and cooler—than the rest of the sun's surface. While the photosphere is normally about 10,000°F (5,500°C), the sunspots average around 3,500°F (1,900°C)—still not exactly brisk! The darkest, coolest part of the sunspot is called the *umbra* ("shadow"). Around the umbra is a gray area called the *penumbra* ("almost shadow"). The penumbra is filled with dark threads called *filaments*.

In 1801, astronomer William Herschel suggested that the sun was a planet, like the earth, though much larger. Sunlight, Herschel claimed, came from glowing clouds in its atmosphere. The sunspots were holes in the clouds through which we could see the dark ground below. Herschel even suggested that there might be beings who lived on the sun.

Not too surprisingly, nobody took Herschel seriously. But other scientists continued their own research into sunspots. In 1908, astronomer George Ellery Hale looked at the sun's light through a spectroscope and discovered that sunspots contained powerful magnetic fields.

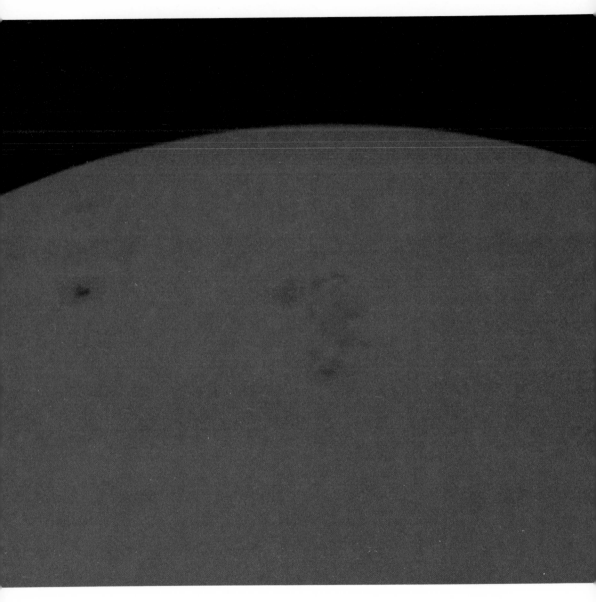

*Sunspots*

This was not completely surprising. Magnetic fields around planets and stars were nothing new. It had been known for a long time that there was a weak magnetic field around the planet earth, for instance, possibly caused by its molten metallic core plus the rapid spinning of the earth on its axis. This is why compass needles always point north. The earth's magnetic field attracts the needle in that direction, just as a small horseshoe magnet might attract a nail. The sun has a magnetic field as well, of about the same strength.

The magnetic field that Hale had detected in sunspots was thousands of times stronger than the earth's magnetic field. It was as though there were a huge electromagnet in the sun. Why? Where would this magnetic field come from?

We saw a moment ago that magnetic fields can be generated by a flow of electricity. And electricity is simply the flow of electrons. Inside the sun, the heat is so great that the electrons are ripped out of the fabric of atoms. Then they run around loose, creating electricity. This electricity, in turn, creates a magnetic field, just as it does in an electromagnet. So, in a very real sense, there *is* a giant electromagnet inside the sun.

The magnetic fields on the sun are huge, many times larger than the entire planet that we live on! They run beneath the sun like long ropes, ropes of magnetic force.

Like the earth, the sun rotates. As it rotates, the gases in its outer layers get stirred up, just as a bowl of oatmeal gets stirred up if you turn it rapidly. This causes the magnetic "ropes" to get tangled. Sometimes they break through the sun's surface, twisting through space like a runaway garden hose. It is possible for a magnetic field to form a giant "arch" over the sun's surface, above the spot where it broke through.

These magnetic fields have a powerful effect on the hot gases around them. The gases become "locked" by the magnetic force, the same way a paper clip becomes trapped by the mild force of a horseshoe magnet. The magnetic field grips the gases in its tight "fist." The hot, glowing gases cannot move.

—43

Heat cannot travel upward from the sun's core. Convective cells cannot rise. Because heat cannot reach them, the gases begin to cool off.

This is how sunspots form. As the gas cools, it grows dimmer. From earth, it appears to be a dark spot. The magnetic arch has two "legs," one for each point where the magnetic field breaks through the sun's surface. At each of these points a sunspot forms, as though the arch were leaving its "footprints" on the sun's surface. This is why sunspots always come in pairs.

The magnetic arch sometimes carries hot gases out into space with it. In fact, when we look through a telescope at the edge of the sun, we can see giant arches of flame rising high above the surface. These are called *prominences*. They are made up of hot, glowing gases trapped in a magnetic field. Though they seem small next to the sun, they are as large or larger than the earth itself! Yet they can rise and fall within hours or even minutes. Sometimes, though, they will remain standing over the sun for weeks at a time.

Occasionally, the magnetic forces will cause explosions on the sun. These explosions, as powerful as a million hydrogen bombs, send huge amounts of heat, light, other forms of radiation, and subatomic particles shooting out into space. These explosions are called *flares*.

Both prominences and flares are directly connected with sunspots and only happen when sunspots are around. We call these events—sunspots, prominences, and flares—the *active,* or *violent, sun.*

Sunspots come in cycles, according to a regular pattern. During the period referred to as the *solar minimum,* they appear very rarely. During the *solar maximum,* sunspots are

*Solar prominences*

—44

quite common. The time period from one solar maximum to the next is usually about eleven years. This is called the *sunspot cycle.*

The sunspot cycle begins when sunspots first appear about 30° north and south of the sun's equator. (This is about one third of the distance from the sun's equator to the poles.) Over the next few years, sunspot pairs (which last only a few weeks each) make appearances closer and closer to the equator. By the time of the solar maximum, sunspots are clustered thickly around the equator. Then they vanish, and the cycle starts all over again.

There is another cycle that sunspots go through. This cycle involves the magnetic fields surrounding the sunspots and is called the *solar magnetic cycle.* The solar magnetic fields go through a series of changes that takes twenty-two years.

No one knows why solar activity follows these eleven- and twenty-two-year patterns. But recent observations have shown that there are bands of moving gas that take twenty-two years to make a trip across the surface of the sun. This may in some way be related to the sunspot and solar magnetic cycles. Perhaps these moving bands serve to tangle the lines of magnetic force that create sunspots.

The sunspot cycle affects not only the sun but also the earth. We'll take a look at this effect in the next chapter.

# CHAPTER SIX
## EARTH AND THE SUN

What contribution does the sun make to the earth?

That's a pretty big question. We can, however, sum up the answer in a single word: *energy*.

As mentioned earlier, energy is what gives us the ability to move. Since you are able to move (as when you turn the pages of this book or even scan your eyes across the page), you must have energy. You get this energy from the food you eat. Since the food on your plate *doesn't* move, you might doubt that it contains energy. The energy in food, though, is in a different form from the energy in your body. Special organs in your body convert that energy into a form you can use.

Anything that moves must have energy. An automobile has energy, which it gets from gasoline. A ball tossed into the air has energy, which it gets from the motion of the thrower's arm. Even moving atoms and atoms combined into larger units of matter called molecules have energy. We have a special word for the motion of individual atoms and molecules. We call it *heat*. Heat is a form of energy.

You may think that heat is what you feel when you stand close to a fire. This is true. You are feeling radiation (infrared radiation) coming from the fire. But you are also feeling the heat of the atoms in motion in the air around you. These atoms get their heat energy from the fire itself.

# The Weather Cycle

Moisture

Rain

Cooler Air

Wind

Warm Air

Where does all this energy—in fire, in food, in gasoline, and so on—come from originally?

From the sun, of course.

The nuclear fusion reactions in the sun produce huge amounts of energy, of which the earth intercepts less than a billionth. Even this small fraction, however, represents a huge amount of energy. The solar energy that falls on 1 square meter of the earth would be enough to heat and light a small room.

This energy comes to us mainly in the form of visible radiation—light—and infrared radiation. Most of this radiation is converted to heat when the sunlight strikes the ground. The ground becomes warm. The heat of the ground radiates into the air.

The process by which this heat spreads through the atmosphere is called *weather.* And the source of the energy that drives the weather is the sun.

When the heat of the ground passes into the air, the atoms in that air begin to move more quickly. (Heat, remember, is the movement of atoms and molecules.) If there is water nearby, the water molecules will also become warm and begin to move quickly. The fast-moving water molecules turn into a gas, water vapor. Then the water vapor mixes with the atoms in the warm air.

Because the atoms in the warm air are energetic and fast-moving, they begin to rise from the ground, letting less energetic—cooler—atoms in the air move down to take their place. (This is why we say that *warm air rises.*) As the air rises, the water vapor rises with it.

The air above the ground is usually cooler than the air next to the ground. This is because the air is not heated directly by sunlight, but by the heat radiated from the ground (which was heated by the sunlight). As air rises, therefore, it becomes cooler. As it becomes cooler, the atoms in the air slow down. So do the molecules in the water vapor. The water vapor turns back into liquid water, forming tiny droplets. Large groups of these droplets form into clouds, floating high above the ground. These droplets sometimes collide with one another, forming larger droplets called raindrops. The result is rain. Snow and other forms of precipitation—hail, sleet, freezing rain, etc.—all form in much the same way. As the warm air rises, more air must move in to take its place. This, in turn, creates wind. All of these weather phenomena, then, are powered by the sun. Their energy comes from the heat energy of the sun.

Because the earth is round, some parts of it get more of this heat than other parts. The section of the earth that gets the most heat is around the middle—the equator.

Because the equator gets more heat than the rest of the earth, you might expect the air to be rising there (because, as we saw a moment ago, warm air rises). And so it is. As the air rises, rain clouds form. (This, by the way, is why the equator is a very rainy place.) Winds rush from the north and south to replace this rising air. These winds are given a twist by the rotation of the earth, so that they tend to blow to the west. We call these the *trade winds*. The sailing ships of Christopher Columbus were pushed across the Atlantic Ocean by these trade winds.

All because of the heat of the sun.

If weather is created by the sun's heat, could changes in the sun cause changes in the weather?

It would seem so.

We saw in the last chapter how sunspots appear and disappear in an eleven-year cycle. A few scientists suspect that this cycle and changes in our weather are closely related. (In fact, a few imaginative and playful theorists have even suggested that sunspots have an effect on such earthly phenomena as politics and the stock market.)

How could sunspots affect the weather? Even those who

have proposed a relationship are hard pressed to explain just what that relationship is. Still, there is evidence that a relationship does exist.

For one thing, the sunspot cycle is not an altogether reliable thing. In the late seventeenth and early eighteenth centuries, over a period of about seventy years, sunspots disappeared almost entirely. The eleven-year cycle practically ceased altogether. This period is called the *Maunder minimum*, after the astronomer who first recognized that it had happened.

By what may or may not have been a coincidence, the Maunder minimum took place at the peak of what has come to be known as the "Little Ice Age." This was a period of several centuries during which temperatures plunged to record lows.

Was this an accident? Solar astronomer John A. Eddy researched sunspot data to see if there were any other periods of unusual sunspot activity.

It is possible to measure the amount of past sunspot activity by looking at the growth rings in very old trees. Certain chemicals are present in tree rings in times of low sunspot activity that are not present during times of high sunspot activity. Eddy analyzed the rings of very old trees and developed a detailed picture of sunspot activity over the last several thousand years. He discovered that there have been many periods of unusually low and unusually high sunspot activity. Furthermore, at least two of these periods corresponded with lengthy spells of unusual weather. According to Eddy, when sunspot activity has been unusually high, the weather has often been unusually warm. And when sunspot activity has been unusually low, the weather has often been unusually cold.

Accident? Coincidence?

Cause and effect?

No one knows for sure, but scientists are busy trying to find out.

This whole train of thought, though, leads us to some frightening conclusions. There have been periods in the distant

*A solar eruption as seen from* Skylab 3.
*The colors in this photograph have been enhanced
by a computer to show important details.*

past when the weather has been quite unlike what it is today. During some of these periods, called *ice ages,* the weather has been extremely cold all over the world. Europe and the northern part of what is now the United States were covered, during ice ages, with great ice fields called *glaciers.* During other periods the weather has been unusually warm. It was during one such period that the dinosaurs lived. Then, when this period ended and the weather cooled, the dinosaurs disappeared, possibly killed off by the sudden chill. (It should be noted, however, that there are other theories concerning the disappearance of the dinosaurs.)

If short periods of unusual weather are linked with short periods of unusual sunspot activity, could long periods of unusual weather (such as ice ages) be linked with long periods of unusual sunspot activity?

Once again, no one knows for sure, but many scientists doubt it. Yet there has been some evidence that changes in the sunspot cycle are connected with changes in the sun's internal temperature, which *could* have an effect on the weather. And, as we shall see in the next chapter, there is also evidence that the sun's internal temperature is unusually low at this very moment!

Are we about to enter a new ice age?

Sunspots may or may not affect the weather. They do, however, have a definite effect on other aspects of earthly life.

We saw in the last chapter that flare explosions take place mostly in times of high sunspot activity. Flares are almost always associated with sunspot groupings.

A flare can send great numbers of particles, including electrons, shooting away from the sun. These particles reach the earth after about two days of traveling through space and become trapped in the earth's magnetic field. They then orbit the earth at high altitudes, forming what are known as the *Van Allen radiation belts.* These radiation belts were discovered by the scientist James Van Allen when he analyzed data from a satellite launch in 1958. Sometimes these particles come close to the earth's surface at the North and South Poles, where the magnetic field is weakest. As they descend through the upper atmosphere, the electric currents generated by them create shimmering curtains of light in the sky. These curtains of light are called *auroras.* The one that appears above the North Pole is called the *aurora borealis* ("northern lights"), and the one that appears above the South Pole is called the *aurora australis* ("southern lights"). During heavy sunspot activity, the northern lights can be seen in much of the northern United States and also in the northernmost parts of Europe.

When the earth is bombarded by a particularly large number of particles, it may produce a phenomenon called a *magnetic storm.* The flow of particles around the earth sets up an intense magnetic field, interfering with radio communications and the generation of electricity. In 1972, a series of solar flares caused a 230,000-volt transformer in British Columbia to explode. Such a magnetic storm could produce widespread power blackouts.

And they'd all be caused by electrons flowing out from the sun.

We said a moment ago that the sun's main (and, in some ways, only) contribution to the earth is energy.

This may seem odd. We see in the newspapers almost every week that there is an energy crisis. We are running out of energy. There isn't enough energy to go around.

How can this be, if our energy is supplied by the sun? Surely the sun has enough energy to supply our needs.

That's true. When we speak of the energy crisis, we are referring only to the energy stored in what we call the *fossil fuels.* Fossil fuels, such as petroleum (from which we get gasoline) and coal, are found underground. They exist in limited supplies.

*The northern lights*

Yet their energy, too, comes from the sun.

There is a special process by which plants can trap the sun's energy and store it in molecules and atoms, somewhat like the way we store electricity in a battery. This process is called *photosynthesis*. Through photosynthesis, plants obtain the energy that allows them to grow. Even plants need energy.

When animals eat these plants, the stored energy enters their bodies. When other animals eat the animals that eat the plants, this energy then enters *their* bodies. Therefore, when you eat broccoli or beef or any other kind of vegetable or meat, you are actually eating the stored energy of the sun.

Fossil fuels are merely plants or animals that have been trapped underground for millions of years, until the pressure of the earth above them has squeezed their stored energy down into a highly concentrated form. Thus, when you put gasoline into the tank of a car, you are again using the stored energy of the sun.

Just about every form of energy that we use on earth relates in some way to the sun. Hydropower uses giant turbines to catch the energy of flowing rivers. These rivers could not flow, however, if rising air and rainstorms did not carry the water back uphill after it flows down. And rainstorms, of course, receive their energy from the sun. Windmills can also be used to generate power. But the wind would not blow and turn the windmills if not for the heat energy of the sun. Even animal power—horse-drawn carriages, for instance, or plows pulled by oxen, or the strength of your own arms and legs— would be impossible without the solar energy stored in food.

The sun has always been the source of energy here on earth. Of all the major types of power generation currently in use, only nuclear power does not depend on the sun's heat. Nuclear power uses certain kinds of highly unstable atoms, which tend to change into other kinds of atoms, releasing energy as they do so. This released energy can be used to heat water and drive steam engines, which in turn can power electric generators.

However, these same unstable atoms were formed in the hearts of stars, stars undergoing huge explosions of a type we'll examine in the next chapter. So, in a sense, nuclear power is also solar power, one generation removed.

In a few more years, it may be possible for human beings to generate power through hydrogen fusion, the same process at work in the sun itself. So-called fusion reactors would heat hydrogen to such tremendous temperatures that it would begin fusing into helium. The main obstacle to this kind of controlled hydrogen fusion is the incredible temperatures involved—temperatures as high as those in the sun. What sort of container could we use to hold the hydrogen ions at temperatures in the millions of degrees? Any kind of solid matter would be vaporized instantly by such heat.

Many scientists believe that the answer is magnetism—that is, the use of a magnetic "bottle" to contain the fusing hydrogen atoms. After all, this is the way powerful magnetic fields on the sun contain the hydrogen ions within a sunspot.

And, if controlled hydrogen fusion can become a reality, we'll have, so to speak, a tiny piece of the sun right here on earth, to do with as we wish.

# CHAPTER SEVEN
# THE DEATH
# OF A STAR

The sun is about 5 billion years old. It should keep shining for another 5 billion years. The life of the sun is about half over.

Or is it?

Is the sun even now running out of fuel?

We saw in chapter three that the sun "burns" hydrogen through a process called fusion. Could this activity be coming to an end? Is the sun burning out, at least temporarily?

No one is sure, but some scientists have started wondering. There is evidence that something unusual is going on inside the sun. This evidence comes from a new kind of astronomy that lets us look past the outer layers of the sun straight through to its core.

Earlier, we learned that atoms are made up of smaller particles. Sometimes these particles are actually knocked out of the atoms. One of these particles, as we saw, is the electron.

Another is the *neutrino*. The neutrino is extremely tiny—so tiny that it may have no weight at all! In fact, the neutrino is so small that it can slip right through ordinary matter, almost as though it weren't there. For this reason, the neutrino is sometimes called a "ghost particle." To stop a neutrino, you would need a wall of lead 600 *trillion* miles (9,600 billion km) thick. Neutrinos travel at very high speeds, too. One could pass through the entire planet earth in a fraction of a second. In fact, at this very moment thousands of neutrinos are passing (without harm to you) right through your body.

Neutrinos are knocked out of atoms during hydrogen fusion. Therefore, there are millions of neutrinos being produced every moment at the sun's core.

The gases at the sun's core are very tightly packed. Gamma rays (which eventually become light rays) take millions of years to reach the sun's surface. (They take only eight minutes to reach the earth from the sun, though the distance is hundreds of times greater.) When we look at the sun in ordinary light, we can get an idea of what things were like at its core millions of years ago, because that was when the light began its journey toward us.

Neutrinos, however, take only a few seconds to travel from the sun's core to its surface. If we could look at the sun in *neutrino light*, we would know what the sun's core is like right now. If we could somehow "see" these tiny particles as they shoot across space, they would tell us many things about the sun.

But neutrinos, unlike ordinary light, would pass through our eyes or our telescopes before we could ever see them. What kind of telescope, then, could we use to look at these invisible ghost particles?

The telescope that astronomers use to "see" neutrinos looks a lot like a vat of cleaning fluid. In fact, it *is* a vat of cleaning fluid. It sits in an old mine in South Dakota, hundreds of feet beneath the ground. Ordinary sunlight cannot reach the neutrino telescope, but neutrinos can. They pass through the solid rock above the telescope like stones falling through water (though they are not even slowed down by the trip).

When the neutrinos pass through the cleaning fluid, they cause it to undergo certain changes. Scientists can detect these changes with sensitive instruments something like Geiger counters. These changes tell them how many neutrinos are presently coming out of the sun.

And there aren't enough.

From what they know about fusion, scientists have a pretty

good idea of how many neutrinos the sun *should* be producing. The number of neutrinos passing through the cleaning fluid, however, is only about a third of this. Where are the rest?

No one knows. Neutrinos, however, are produced by hydrogen fusion. Maybe the fusion inside the sun has somehow stopped, turned itself off.

Would this mean the end of our world? The sun is our main source of light and heat here on earth. Without it, our planet would be a frozen snowball of a world. If the sun has shut itself off, are we doomed?

Not necessarily. For one thing, it would probably be many years before it had much effect on us. The sun's heat takes millions of years to travel from the core to the earth. Furthermore, this "solar shutdown," if that is what this is, may be only temporary. One theory suggests that the sun's core sometimes gets clogged with helium—the "ashes" of hydrogen fusion burning. These ashes must be cleared out before the sun can continue burning.

There may be a connection between the missing neutrinos and the sunspot cycle, which means that there may also be a connection between neutrinos and ice ages. The evidence is not accepted by all scientists, but it is very interesting nonetheless. Sunspots may indicate that hydrogen fusion is going on inside the sun. If there are no sunspots, then there may also be no fusion. The Maunder minimum was a period when there were no sunspots. Is this why temperatures went down all over the earth during the Maunder minimum—because there was no fusion inside the sun? Does this explain why ice ages are related to sunspot minimums? Do the missing solar neutrinos mean that a new ice age is on the way?

Only time will tell.

Whether or not hydrogen fusion is currently going on at its core, the sun will probably live to a ripe old age. When it *does* run out of hydrogen, will our sun die?

Yes, but not right away. Without hydrogen fusion, the sun will no longer be able to resist its own gravity. It will literally collapse under its own weight. But as the sun collapses, its atoms will jam up against one another and begin producing heat energy through gravitational friction—the friction of atom against atom—just as it did when it was first formed. This time, the sun will become so hot that something new will start to happen—*helium* fusion. Helium atoms will fuse together to create even larger atoms.

Helium fusion will release even more energy than hydrogen fusion, and this will keep the sun burning very hotly for another million years or so. The heat from the core will cause the outer layers of the sun to balloon out to hundreds of times their original size. The sun will become a bloated *red giant*, so-called because of its size and the fact that it will glow a dull-red color.

This red giant will swallow up all of the inner planets—Mercury, Venus, perhaps even the earth and Mars. Life on earth will no longer be possible. Fortunately for us, this won't happen for 5 billion years yet.

The red giant will use up its helium fuel very quickly. Then it will start collapsing again. It will collapse until all of the atoms are again jammed up against one another, this time in an even tighter mass. The sun will then be about as large as the earth. It will be so dense and tightly packed that one cubic inch of solar matter will weigh more than a ton!

This kind of collapsed star is called a *white dwarf*.

The surface of the white dwarf will be very hot, hotter than the surface of the sun today. It will be very bright as well. But the white dwarf itself will be very small. From earth (or from where the earth used to be), it will look very dim and far away.

The collapsed sun, however, will not produce any new heat. It will be dead. After a few billion years, it will cool off and go dark. It will become a *black dwarf*. And that will be the end of our sun.

Other stars have ended their lives more dramatically than our sun will. Very large and massive stars die in a tremendous explosion called a *supernova.* For a few days or weeks, the supernova produces as much light and heat as a hundred billion stars! One supernova can be as bright as an entire galaxy!

Actually, if it were not for a supernova that took place billions of years ago, our sun might not exist today.

We saw earlier that the sun formed out of a collapsing cloud of hydrogen. But why did that cloud collapse?

Scientists say that gravity caused the atoms of gas to move closer together. But there is a flaw in this theory. The cloud of hydrogen was very stable. That is, it would not have collapsed on its own. The atoms of gas were spread out very evenly throughout the cloud. So was their gravity. All of the atoms would have been experiencing equal gravitational pull from all directions. Like two evenly matched teams in a tug-of-war, the gravitational forces would have balanced one another out. The cloud shouldn't have collapsed.

But it did.

Astronomers now believe that there was a supernova about 5 billion years ago, near where the sun is now. Next to this exploding star was a huge cloud of hydrogen gas. The supernova explosion sent waves rippling through this cloud, just as a passing motorboat sends waves rippling through water. The waves crushed sections of the cloud. One of these sections became so crushed that the balance of gravity became upset. This section became unstable. It began to collapse. This part of the cloud became our sun.

*The chromosphere of the sun
(pink color) shows through in
this solar telescope photograph
of an eclipse of the sun.*

We've seen how hydrogen atoms fuse together to create helium atoms. Helium atoms can fuse together into even larger atoms. In the incredible heat of a supernova explosion, all kinds of atoms can fuse together into all other kinds of atoms. In fact, this is how all of the different kinds of atoms on our planet—representing nearly 100 different elements, including gases and metals—were created. The atoms in this book, in your house, even the atoms in your body were all created in a supernova explosion during which simple atoms were combined together at high temperatures.

Probably, the elements of the planet earth were formed in the very explosion that we just talked about, the one that triggered the collapse of the hydrogen cloud that became our sun.

So, in a very real sense, we owe the birth of our sun—and of life itself—to the death of a star.

# *GLOSSARY*

**Atoms**—the basic building blocks of matter. Everything in the universe (with a few very rare exceptions) is made up of atoms.

**Black dwarf**—a white dwarf (collapsed star) that has cooled off—in effect, died.

**Centrifugal force**—a force that tends to push something outward from a center of rotation; acts to counterbalance the force of gravity.

**Chromosphere**—("sphere of colors") the lowest level of the sun's atmosphere. Glows with a faint pinkish light.

**Corona**—a bright cloud of hot gases surrounding the sun.

**Eclipse**—apparent darkening of the sun's disk that takes place when the moon moves between the earth and the sun. You should never look at the sun directly, even during an eclipse. It can cause blindness.

**Electron**—one of the subatomic particles that makes up the atom. Electricity is simply the flow of electrons.

**Energy**—the property that makes things move. Anything in motion can be said to possess energy. (Under certain conditions, objects that are not moving are said to possess *potential energy*, if that object can start moving without gaining new energy.)

**Flare**—explosion on the sun; related to sunspots.

**Galaxy**—a "star island"; a group of stars that travels through space together. The *Milky Way* is our own galaxy.

**Gamma rays**—an invisible form of radiation, very hot and very energetic.

**Gravitation**—also called *gravity*; the force that attracts every object in the universe to every other object; the "glue" that holds planets in orbit around stars and moons in orbit around planets.

**Gravitational collapse**—the way in which stars form. Atoms of hydrogen are pulled together by gravity, creating heat through a kind of friction, until the hydrogen is hot enough for fusion to start.

**Heliocentric model of the universe**—the model of the solar system that has the sun at the center, with the planets revolving around it.

**Hydrogen fusion**—under extremely high temperatures, hydrogen atoms will fuse together (combine) into helium atoms. This releases energy in the form of gamma rays.

**Ions**—atoms that have lost or gained electrons. Unlike ordinary atoms, ions have an electric charge.

**Magnetic fields**—regions of space through which magnetism exerts its force. Any magnet is surrounded by a magnetic field. An electric current can produce a magnetic field.

**Neutrino**—a kind of subatomic particle so small that it may not have any weight at all. Sometimes referred to as a "ghost particle" because it can pass through solid matter.

**Photon**—a particle of light that travels in the form of a wave.

**Photosphere**—the "surface" of the sun. The photosphere is the brightly lit part of the sun that we see from earth.

**Photosynthesis**—the process whereby green plants are able to make their own food using sunlight as a raw material.

**Prominence**—giant "arcs" of flame rising high above the surface of the sun. These arcs are made up of hot, glowing gases trapped in a magnetic field.

**Radiation**—the energy-carrying waves that radiate (move outward) from a central source. Though radiation is a wave, under certain conditions it can also take the form of particles.

**Red giant**—a star that has used up all of its hydrogen and swelled to an enormous size due to the helium fusion taking place.

**Solar system**—the family of planets and other orbiting objects that circle the sun, held in place by the sun's gravity.

**Spectrograph**—an instrument for dispersing radiation into a spectrum; used to detect what elements are present in a star, the temperature of the star, etc.

**Subatomic particles**—particles that are smaller than the atom.

**Sunspot cycle**—a period of roughly eleven years during which sunspots increase in frequency, then disappear.

**Sunspots**—relatively black and cool areas on the surface of the sun, created by runaway magnetic fields.

**White dwarf**—a collapsed star; what happens to a red giant when it has used up all of its helium fuel.

**Winter solstice**—the time of year when the sun starts to move northward again. The first day of winter in the northern hemisphere.

**Yellow dwarf**—an average-size, middle-aged star, like our sun.

# FOR FURTHER READING

Adams, Florence. *Catch a Sunbeam.* New York: Harcourt Brace Javonovich, 1978.

Branley, Franklyn M. *The Sun: Star Number One.* New York: T.Y. Crowell, 1964.

Gallant, Roy A. *Fires in the Sky.* New York: Four Winds Press, 1978.

Hey, Nigel S. *The Mysterious Sun.* New York: G.P. Putnam's Sons, 1971.

Jaber, William. *Exploring the Sun.* New York: Julian Messner, 1980.

Weart, Spencer R. *How to Build a Sun.* New York: Coward-McCann, 1970.

# INDEX

# ABOUT
# THE AUTHOR

Christopher Lampton is a free-lance writer who specializes in writing about science subjects. He is a former radio announcer and producer of television commercials, with a degree in broadcasting and communications. He is the author of two Impact books for Franklin Watts, called *Black Holes and Other Secrets of the Universe* and *Meteorology: An Introduction*, and is currently at work on a book about fusion energy.

Mr. Lampton makes his home in Hyattsville, Maryland, just outside of Washington, D.C.